Riches to Truest Riches!

12 Word-Based Principles for Enriching Your Life with True Riches

Rev. Dr. Walter A. McCray
Gospelizer

BLACK LIGHT FELLOWSHIP
A Beacon of Christ

Chicago, Illinois

Riches to Truest Riches!
12 Word-Based Principles for Enriching Your Life with True Riches
Rev. Dr. Walter Arthur McCray

BLACK LIGHT FELLOWSHIP
A Beacon of Christ

P.O. Box 5369 • Chicago, IL 60680
Ph. 773.826.7790 • Fax 773.826.7792
Email: info@blacklightfellowship.com

https://www.BlackLightFellowship.com

ISBN: 978-0-933176-31-7
Copyright ©1994, 2020 Walter Arthur McCray.
All Rights Reserved.
All copying, electronic or otherwise, is prohibited.

Editorial Services
Mary C. Lewis, MCL Editing, Etc., Evanston, IL
mclwriter@msn.com

Cover & Design Services
Michelle D. Muhammad, MDM Design, Chicago, IL
mdm_621@yahoo.com

Scripture quotations marked (NLT) are taken from the Holy Bible, New Living Translation, copyright ©1996, 2004, 2015 by Tyndale House Foundation. Used by permission of Tyndale House Publishers, a Division of Tyndale House Ministries, Carol Stream, Illinois 60188. All rights reserved.

Scripture quotations marked (NIV) are taken from the Holy Bible, New International Version®, NIV®. Copyright © 1973, 1978, 1984, 2011 by Biblica, Inc.™ Used by permission of Zondervan. All rights reserved worldwide. www.zondervan.com The "NIV" and "New International Version" are trademarks registered in the United States Patent and Trademark Office by Biblica, Inc.™

Scripture quotations marked (CEV) are from the Contemporary English Version Copyright © 1991, 1992, 1995 by American Bible Society. Used by Permission.

Scripture quotations marked (NKJV) are taken from the New King James Version®. Copyright © 1982 by Thomas Nelson. Used by permission. All rights reserved.

Printed in the USA

Riches to Truest Riches!

12 Word-Based Principles for Enriching Your Life with True Riches

"So if you have not been trustworthy in handling worldly wealth, who will trust you with true riches?"

— Jesus Christ
Luke 16:11, *NIV*

Riches to Truest Riches!

- **Riches** are "valuable possessions"; "abundant and precious things"; "wealth and treasure".[1]
- **Riches**, as things of value, are present *with* or *within* you.
- **Riches** vary; your wealth may be financial, material, social, internal, intellectual, spiritual, eternal, or some other valuable possession or thing you control.
  > **What riches do you see in your life?**

- **Riches** given are *a greater blessing* than riches received.
  > **How do you share precious things with others?**

- **Riches** of the truest kind are treasures with *a lasting value*, and the greatest of all the valuables in life.
  > **What are your very best treasures?**

- **Riches** can abundantly *grow* in your life experience into *true* riches, as taught by Jesus Christ.
  > **In what ways are you growing your true riches?**

- **Riches to Truest Riches!** gives you a simple process for gaining true riches. Use its insights to identify, care for, wisely use, and increase your personal riches. Here is help for growing the wealth of your life into precious things of the *best* value. Motivate yourself to *bless others* by spreading around your most valuable treasures. Act on these 12 Word-based principles to abundantly *enrich yourself* with the *truest* valuables of your life!

[1] See "riches" at Merriam-Webster.com, thefreedictionary.com, Dictionary.com.

Riches

1. *Specify*
2. *Sort*
3. *Survey*
4. *Sanctify*
5. *Secure*
6. *Shut Off*
7. *Save*
8. *Spend*
9. *Share*
10. *Show*
11. *Sell*
12. *Sprout*

Truest Riches!

~ 1ˢᵗ ~
Specify
your riches to focus.

✼ Identify your riches by taking an inventory of all you have and oversee. Bring your riches into focus. Spotlight and understand your personal giftedness, the treasures you possess and control, and the good impact of your influence. Attempt to clearly see your worth, and the wealth of your things and experience. Name your valuables. Describe the financial, material, social, internal, intellectual, spiritual, eternal, and other precious things in your life. Be thankful to God for all your riches, for these treasures are gifts from above.

◆ financial, material, social, internal, intellectual,
spiritual, and eternal things of value ◆

★ "[17] He did all this so you would never say to yourself, 'I have achieved this wealth with my own strength and energy.' [18] Remember the LORD your God. He is the one who gives you power to be

successful, in order to fulfill the covenant he confirmed to your ancestors with an oath." (Deuteronomy 8:17–18, *NLT*)

✶ "The blessing of the Lord makes a person rich, and he adds no sorrow with it." (Proverbs 10:22, *NLT*)

✶ "And it is a good thing to receive wealth from God and the good health to enjoy it. To enjoy your work and accept your lot in life—this is indeed a gift from God." (Ecclesiastes 5:19, *NLT*)

✶ "⁷O God, I beg two favors from you; let me have them before I die. ⁸First, help me never to tell a lie. Second, give me neither poverty nor riches! Give me just enough to satisfy my needs. ⁹For if I grow rich, I may deny you and say, 'Who is the Lord?' And if I am too poor, I may steal and thus insult God's holy name." (Proverbs 30:7–9, *NLT*)

✶ "³⁸'How much bread do you have?' he asked. 'Go and find out.' They came back and reported, 'We have five loaves of bread and two fish.' ³⁹Then Jesus told the disciples to have the people sit down in groups on the green grass. ⁴⁰So they sat down in groups of fifty or a hundred. ⁴¹Jesus took the five loaves and two fish, looked up toward heaven, and blessed them. Then, breaking the loaves into pieces, he kept giving the bread to the disciples so they could distribute it to the people. He also divided the fish for everyone to share. ⁴²They all ate as much as they wanted, ⁴³and afterward, the disciples picked up twelve baskets of leftover bread and fish. ⁴⁴A total of 5,000 men and their families were fed." (Mark 6:38–44, *NLT*)

✶ "¹Now Peter and John went up together to the temple at the hour of prayer, the ninth hour. ²And a certain man lame from his mother's womb was carried, whom they laid daily at the gate of the temple which is called Beautiful, to ask alms from those who entered the temple; ³who, seeing Peter and John about to go into the temple, asked for alms. ⁴And fixing his eyes on him, with John, Peter said, 'Look at us.' ⁵So he gave them his attention, expecting to receive something from them. ⁶Then Peter said, 'Silver and gold I do not have, but what I do have I give you: In the name of Jesus Christ of Nazareth, rise up and walk.' ⁷And he took him by the right hand and lifted him up, and immediately his feet and ankle bones received strength." (Acts 3:1–7, *NKJV*)

✶ "He is so rich in kindness and grace that he purchased our freedom with the blood of his Son and forgave our sins." (Ephesians 1:7, *NLT*)

★ "I pray that your hearts will be flooded with light so that you can understand the confident hope he has given to those he called—his holy people who are his rich and glorious inheritance." (Ephesians 1:18, *NLT*)

★ "⁶Now godliness with contentment is great gain. ⁷For we brought nothing into this world, and it is certain we can carry nothing out. ⁸And having food and clothing, with these we shall be content." (1 Timothy 6:6–8, *NKJV*)

★ "In him lie hidden all the treasures of wisdom and knowledge." (Colossians 2:3, *NLT*)

★ "Whatever is good and perfect is a gift coming down to us from God our Father, who created all the lights in the heavens. He never changes or casts a shifting shadow." (James 1:17, *NLT*)

★ "¹⁸For you know that God paid a ransom to save you from the empty life you inherited from your ancestors. And it was not paid with mere gold or silver, which lose their value. ¹⁹It was the precious blood of Christ, the sinless, spotless Lamb of God." (1 Peter 1:18–19, *NLT*)

★ "You claim to be rich and successful and to have everything you need. But you don't know how bad off you are. You are pitiful, poor, blind, and naked." (Revelation 3:17, *CEV*)

~2nd~
Sort

your riches into workable groups.

✳ Classify your riches into categories that work for you, according to their kind, worth, and usefulness. Your initial impression of the relative value of your gifts will help you to assign them to their group. Consider sorting your riches good to best, material to spiritual, personal to social, temporary to lasting, or the like. This sorting process is dynamic; so, from time to time you may change how you classify your valuables.

◆ financial, material, social, internal, intellectual, spiritual, and eternal things of value ◆

★ "That is why I tell you not to worry about everyday life—whether you have enough food and drink, or enough clothes to wear. Isn't life more than food, and your body more than clothing?" (Matthew 6:25, *NLT*)

✶ "Seek the Kingdom of God above all else, and live righteously, and he will give you everything you need." (Matthew 6:33, *NLT*)

✶ "No one can serve two masters. For you will hate one and love the other; you will be devoted to one and despise the other. You cannot serve God and be enslaved to money." (Luke 16:13, *NLT*)

✶ "Do not trust in extortion or put vain hope in stolen goods; though your riches increase, do not set your heart on them." (Psalm 62:10, *NIV*)

✶ "¹²So I decided to compare wisdom with foolishness and madness (for who can do this better than I, the king?). ¹³I thought, 'Wisdom is better than foolishness, just as light is better than darkness.'" (Ecclesiastes 2:12–13, *NLT*)

✶ "If you love money and wealth, you will never be satisfied with what you have. This doesn't make sense either." (Ecclesiastes 5:10, *CEV*)

✶ "A good reputation is more valuable than costly perfume. And the day you die is better than the day you are born." (Ecclesiastes 7:1, *NLT*)

✶ "²³This is what the LORD says: 'Don't let the wise boast in their wisdom, or the powerful boast in their power, or the rich boast in their riches. ²⁴But those who wish to boast should boast in this alone:

that they truly know me and understand that I am the Lord who demonstrates unfailing love and who brings justice and righteousness to the earth, and that I delight in these things. I, the Lord, have spoken!'" (Jeremiah 9:23–24, *NLT*)

✸ "⁹But those who desire to be rich fall into temptation and a snare, and into many foolish and harmful lusts which drown men in destruction and perdition. ¹⁰For the love of money is a root of all kinds of evil, for which some have strayed from the faith in their greediness, and pierced themselves through with many sorrows." (1 Timothy 6:9–10, *NKJV*)

✸ "²⁵He chose to share the oppression of God's people instead of enjoying the fleeting pleasures of sin. ²⁶He thought it was better to suffer for the sake of Christ than to own the treasures of Egypt, for he was looking ahead to his great reward." (Hebrews 11:25–26, *NLT*)

✸ "These trials will show that your faith is genuine. It is being tested as fire tests and purifies gold—though your faith is far more precious than mere gold. So when your faith remains strong through many trials, it will bring you much praise and glory and honor on the day when Jesus Christ is revealed to the whole world." (1 Peter 1:7, *NLT*)

~ 3rd ~
Survey
your riches for their value.

❋ Look carefully at your riches to ascertain their true worth. Begin thinking a little deeper about the specific riches that you sorted into each category. Highlight your distinctive riches, your special gifts and outstanding abilities. Seriously examine all your personal treasures; be thorough. Make a good and fair appraisal of the wealth that you possess and assign an appropriate value to each of your riches. Neither overestimate nor underestimate your valuables. If necessary, solicit the insightful viewpoint of a trusted friend to assist in evaluating your riches.

♦ financial, material, social, internal, intellectual, spiritual, and eternal things of value ♦

★ "[23] Know the state of your flocks, and put your heart into caring for your herds, [24] for riches don't last forever, and the crown might not be passed to the next generation." (Proverbs 27:23–24, *NLT*)

★ "Who can find a virtuous and capable wife? She is more precious than rubies." (Proverbs 31:10, *NLT*)

★ "¹⁴After Lot had gone, the Lord said to Abram, 'Look as far as you can see in every direction—north and south, east and west. ¹⁵I am giving all this land, as far as you can see, to you and your descendants as a permanent possession. ¹⁶And I will give you so many descendants that, like the dust of the earth, they cannot be counted! ¹⁷Go and walk through the land in every direction, for I am giving it to you.'" (Genesis 13:14–17, *NLT*)

★ "¹But Moses protested again, 'What if they won't believe me or listen to me? What if they say, 'The Lord never appeared to you'?' ²Then the Lord asked him, 'What is that in your hand?' 'A shepherd's staff,' Moses replied. ³'Throw it down on the ground,' the Lord told him. So Moses threw down the staff, and it turned into a snake! Moses jumped back. ⁴Then the Lord told him, 'Reach out and grab its tail.' So Moses reached out and grabbed it, and it turned back into a shepherd's staff in his hand. ⁵'Perform this sign,' the Lord told him. 'Then they will believe that the Lord, the God of their ancestors—the God of

Abraham, the God of Isaac, and the God of Jacob—really has appeared to you.'" (Exodus 4:1–5, *NLT*)

✴ "'The Lord who rescued me from the claws of the lion and the bear will rescue me from this Philistine!' Saul finally consented. 'All right, go ahead,' he said. 'And may the Lord be with you!'" (1 Samuel 17:37, *NLT*)

✴ "Lord, remind me how brief my time on earth will be. Remind me that my days are numbered—how fleeting my life is." (Psalm 39:4, *NLT*)

✴ "The seeds that fell among the thornbushes are also people who hear the message. But they start worrying about the needs of this life and are fooled by the desire to get rich. So the message gets choked out, and they never produce anything." (Matthew 13:22, *CEV*)

✴ "For bodily exercise profits a little, but godliness is profitable for all things, having promise of the life that now is and of that which is to come." (1 Timothy 4:8, *NKJV*)

✴ "Because of the privilege and authority God has given me, I give each of you this warning: Don't think you are better than you really are. Be honest in your evaluation of yourselves, measuring yourselves by the faith God has given us." (Romans 12:3, *NLT*)

-4th-
Sanctify
your riches to the Lord.

Treat your riches as special, as holy possessions. Appreciate the gifts of your personhood, and never devalue or despise your goods. Consecrate your riches to the Lord by giving the first fruits and the tithe of your possessions. Devote your treasures for serving others and improving their lives. Especially dedicate your riches to enhance the people you care for the most. Highly regard your spiritual and eternal valuables. Pray over all your wealth, asking God to sanctify your possessions and to bestow upon you His favor. Give thanks to the Lord and seek His guidance in everything.

♦ financial, material, social, internal, intellectual, spiritual, and eternal things of value ♦

✶ "So teach us to number our days, That we may gain a heart of wisdom." (Psalm 90:12, *NKJV*)

✶ "^{11} So if you have not been trustworthy in handling worldly wealth, who will trust you with true riches? ^{12} And if you have not been trustworthy with someone else's property, who will give you property of your own?" (Luke 16:11–12, *NIV*)

✶ "^{18} King Melchizedek of Salem was a priest of God Most High. He brought out some bread and wine ^{19} and said to Abram: 'I bless you in the name of God Most High, Creator of heaven and earth. ^{20} All praise belongs to God Most High for helping you defeat your enemies.' Then Abram gave Melchizedek a tenth of everything." (Genesis 14:18–20, *CEV*)

✶ "^{20} Jacob solemnly promised God, 'If you go with me and watch over me as I travel, and if you give me food and clothes ^{21} and bring me safely home again, you will be my God. ^{22} This rock will be your house, and I will give back to you a tenth of everything you give me.'" (Genesis 28:20–22, *CEV*)

✶ "I am the LORD All-Powerful, and I challenge you to put me to the test. Bring the entire ten percent into the storehouse, so there will be food in my house. Then I will open the windows of heaven and flood you with blessing after blessing." (Malachi 3:10, *CEV*)

✶ "^{5} Let your conduct be without covetousness; be content with such things as you have. For He Himself has said, 'I will never leave you nor forsake you.' ⁶ So we may boldly say: 'The LORD is my helper; I will not fear. What can man do to me?'" (Hebrews 13:5–6, *NKJV*)

★ "¹⁶ Watch out for immoral and ungodly people like Esau, who sold his future blessing for only one meal. ¹⁷ You know how he later wanted it back. But there was nothing he could do to change things, even though he begged his father and cried." (Hebrews 12:16–17, *CEV*)

★ "¹ Dear friends, God is good. So I beg you to offer your bodies to him as a living sacrifice, pure and pleasing. That's the most sensible way to serve God. ² Don't be like the people of this world, but let God change the way you think. Then you will know how to do everything that is good and pleasing to him." (Romans 12:1–2, *CEV*)

★ "I pray that God, who gives peace, will make you completely holy. And may your spirit, soul, and body be kept healthy and faultless until our Lord Jesus Christ returns." (1 Thessalonians 5:23, *CEV*)

~ 5th ~

Secure

your riches for safekeeping.

Keep your riches safe; whatever they are, protect them. Be sure to collect for the riches that you earn or deserve. Redeem the riches you bought; possess what you are promised. Get insurance on yourself and possessions, and keep the policies current. Value and nurture your friendships and safeguard your close relationships. Maintain the rich vitality of your body and mind, heart, and soul. Prioritize how you use your time—it is precious—and shield your hours and days from wasteful invasions.

◆ financial, material, social, internal, intellectual, spiritual, and eternal things of value ◆

✶ "[20] But God said to him, 'You fool! You will die this very night. Then who will get everything you worked for?' [21] 'Yes, a person is a fool to store up earthly wealth but not have a rich relationship with God.'" (Luke 12:20–21, *NLT*)

✴ "Hezekiah was very wealthy and highly honored. He built special treasury buildings for his silver, gold, precious stones, and spices, and for his shields and other valuable items." (2 Chronicles 32:27, *NLT*)

✴ "[14] Then I looked things over and told the leaders, the officials, and the rest of the people, 'Don't be afraid of your enemies! The Lord is great and fearsome. So think of him and fight for your relatives and children, your wives and homes!' . . . . [21] Every day from dawn to dark, half of the workers rebuilt the walls, while the rest stood guard with their spears." (Nehemiah 4:14, 21, *CEV*)

✴ "A priest descended from Aaron is to accompany the Levites when they receive the tithes, and the Levites are to bring a tenth of the tithes up to the house of our God, to the storerooms of the treasury." (Nehemiah 10:38, *NIV*)

✴ "Above all else, guard your heart, for it is the wellspring of life." (Proverbs 4:23, *NIV*)

✴ "Here's the lesson: Use your worldly resources to benefit others and make friends. Then, when your possessions are gone, they will welcome you to an eternal home." (Luke 16:9, *NLT*)

✷ "Timothy, guard what God has entrusted to you. Avoid godless, foolish discussions with those who oppose you with their so-called knowledge." (1 Timothy 6:20, *NLT*)

✷ "That is why I am suffering here in prison. But I am not ashamed of it, for I know the one in whom I trust, and I am sure that he is able to guard what I have entrusted to him until the day of his return." (2 Timothy 1:12, *NLT*)

✷ "[3] All praise to God, the Father of our Lord Jesus Christ. It is by his great mercy that we have been born again, because God raised Jesus Christ from the dead. Now we live with great expectation, [4] and we have a priceless inheritance—an inheritance that is kept in heaven for you, pure and undefiled, beyond the reach of change and decay. [5] And through your faith, God is protecting you by his power until you receive this salvation, which is ready to be revealed on the last day for all to see." (1 Peter 1:3–5, *NLT*)

✷ "[10] So, dear brothers and sisters, work hard to prove that you really are among those God has called and chosen. Do these things, and you will never fall away. [11] Then God will give you a grand entrance into the eternal Kingdom of our Lord and Savior Jesus Christ." (2 Peter 1:10–11, *NLT*)

~6th~
Shut Off
your riches from takers.

✤ Stop flowing your riches to irresponsible persons who are hoarding or wasting your precious valuables. Protect the health of your wealth. Seasons come when you should cease spending, cease sharing, cease showing, or cease selling your truest riches to leeches. Disconnect your valuables from a wasteful siphon; safeguard your emotional and intellectual gifts from an abusive drainer of your feelings and brain. Don't be intimidated or guilt-ridden, or ashamed to say, "Enough is enough!" Whether your treasurable giving is financial, material, intellectual, or spiritual, when dealing with parasites, you are wise to dispense "No more!"

♦ financial, material, social, internal, intellectual, spiritual, and eternal things of value ♦

★ "'Do not give dogs what is sacred; do not throw your pearls to pigs. If you do, they may trample them under their feet, and turn and tear you to pieces." (Matthew 7:6, *NIV*)

★ "²⁴ But since you refuse to listen when I call and no one pays attention when I stretch out my hand, ²⁵ since you disregard all my advice and do not accept my rebuke, I in turn will laugh when disaster strikes you; ²⁶ I will mock when calamity overtakes you—²⁷ when calamity overtakes you like a storm, when disaster sweeps over you like a whirlwind, when distress and trouble overwhelm you. ²⁸ 'Then they will call to me but I will not answer; they will look for me but will not find me, ²⁹ since they hated knowledge and did not choose to fear the LORD. ³⁰ Since they would not accept my advice and spurned my rebuke, ³¹ they will eat the fruit of their ways and be filled with the fruit of their schemes." (Proverbs 1:24–31, *NIV*)

★ "¹ I will sing for the one I love a song about his vineyard: My loved one had a vineyard on a fertile hillside. ² He dug it up and cleared it of stones and planted it with the choicest vines. He built a watchtower in it and cut out a winepress as well. Then he looked for a crop of good grapes, but it yielded only bad fruit. ³ 'Now you dwellers in Jerusalem and people of Judah, judge between me and my vineyard. ⁴ What more could have been done for my vineyard than I have done for it? When I looked for good grapes, why did it yield only bad? ⁵ Now I will tell you what I am going to do to my vineyard: I will take away its hedge, and it will be destroyed; I will break down its wall, and it will be trampled. ⁶ I will make it a wasteland, neither pruned nor cultivated, and briers and thorns will grow there. I will command the clouds not to rain on it.'" (Isaiah 5:1–6, *NIV*)

✶ "²⁴ 'Then he who had received the one talent came and said, 'Lord, I knew you to be a hard man, reaping where you have not sown, and gathering where you have not scattered seed. ²⁵ And I was afraid, and went and hid your talent in the ground. Look, *there* you have *what is* yours.' ²⁶ 'But his lord answered and said to him, 'You wicked and lazy servant, you knew that I reap where I have not sown, and gather where I have not scattered seed. ²⁷ So you ought to have deposited my money with the bankers, and at my coming I would have received back my own with interest. ²⁸ So take the talent from him, and give it to him who has ten talents. ²⁹ 'For to everyone who has, more will be given, and he will have abundance; but from him who does not have, even what he has will be taken away. ³⁰ And cast the unprofitable servant into the outer darkness. There will be weeping and gnashing of teeth.'" (Matthew 25:24–30, *NKJV*)

✴ "⁴Yet I hold this against you: You have forsaken the love you had at first. ⁵Consider how far you have fallen! Repent and do the things you did at first. If you do not repent, I will come to you and remove your lampstand from its place." (Revelation 2:4–5, *NIV*)

~7th~
Save
your riches for a reserve.

Don't use up all your riches, or exhaust them at once. Keep a reserve, always. Carefully retain a supply of riches to spend, share, and sell. Bank a stash of your riches for tomorrow—for those sunny days, or the rainy days that will surely come. Preserve your strength and, if your health fails, restore it to goodness. Don't waste your valuables, or unnecessarily put them at risk. Plan to leave an inheritance or legacy for the generation succeeding you.

◆ financial, material, social, internal, intellectual, spiritual, and eternal things of value ◆

★ "[19] Don't store up treasures on earth! Moths and rust can destroy them, and thieves can break in and steal them. [20] Instead, store up your treasures in heaven, where moths and rust cannot destroy them, and thieves cannot break in and steal them. [21] Your heart will always be where your treasure is." (Matthew 6:19–21, *CEV*)

✴ "Invest in truth and wisdom, discipline and good sense, and don't part with them." (Proverbs 23:23, *CEV*)

✴ "[6] You lazy people can learn by watching an anthill. [7] Ants don't have leaders, [8] but they store up food during harvest season." (Proverbs 6:6–8, *CEV*)

✴ "[24] On this earth four things are small but very wise: [25] Ants, who seem to be feeble, but store up food all summer long;" (Proverbs 30:24–25, *CEV*)

✴ "[34] Then appoint some other officials to collect one-fifth of every crop harvested in Egypt during the seven years when there is plenty. [35] Give them the power to collect the grain during those good years and to store it in your cities. [36] It can be stored until it is needed during the seven years when there won't be enough grain in Egypt. This will keep the country from being destroyed because of the lack of food." (Genesis 41:34–36, *CEV*)

✴ "Money wrongly gotten will disappear bit by bit; money earned little by little will grow and grow." (Proverbs 13:11, *CEV*)

✶ "Be sensible and store up precious treasures—don't waste them like a fool." (Proverbs 21:20, *CEV*)

✶ "If you obey God, you will have something to leave your grandchildren. If you don't obey God, those who live right will get what you leave." (Proverbs 13:22, *CEV*)

~ 8th ~
Spend
your riches for your good.

✼ Put your riches to work by using precious resources to meet your needs. Expend personal things of value such as your spirit, mind, energies, and time for your overall good and well-being. Use your wealth to purchase things of lasting value. Spend your riches on good things in the right season, anticipating the future. Be on the lookout for opportunities to enrich your treasures. Attain, acquire, and freely buy riches that are more precious than your present valuables.

◆ financial, material, social, internal, intellectual, spiritual, and eternal things of value ◆

✶ "⁶The man answered, 'She is the one who came back from Moab with Naomi. ⁷She asked if she could pick up grain left by the harvest workers, and she has been working all morning without a moment's rest.'" (Ruth 2:6–7, *CEV*)

✶ "But David answered, 'No! I have to pay you what they're worth. I can't offer the LORD my God a sacrifice that I got for nothing.' So David bought the threshing place and the oxen for fifty pieces of silver." (2 Samuel 24:24, *CEV*)

✶ "²⁴The best thing we can do is to enjoy eating, drinking, and working. I believe these are God's gifts to us, ²⁵ and no one enjoys eating and living more than I do." (Ecclesiastes 2:24–25, *CEV*)

✶ "¹² I know the best thing we can do is to always enjoy life, ¹³ because God's gift to us is the happiness we get from our food and drink and from the work we do." (Ecclesiastes 3:12–13, *CEV*)

✶ "¹⁶ She knows how to buy land and how to plant a vineyard, ¹⁷ and she always works hard. ¹⁸ She knows when to buy or sell, and she stays busy until late at night." (Proverbs 31:16–18, *CEV*)

✶ "¹ If you are thirsty, come and drink water! If you don't have any money, come, eat what you want! Drink wine and milk without paying a cent. ² Why waste your money on what really isn't food? Why work hard for something that doesn't satisfy? Listen carefully to me, and you will enjoy the very best foods. ³ Pay close attention! Come to me and live. I will promise you the eternal love and loyalty that I promised David." (Isaiah 55:1–3, *CEV*)

✶ "Buy your gold from me. It has been refined in a fire, and it will make you rich. Buy white clothes from me. Wear them and you can cover up your shameful nakedness. Buy medicine for your eyes, so that you will be able to see." (Revelation 3:18, *CEV*)

~9th~
Share
your riches with compassion.

❦ Care for others with your riches, spread them around. Bless those whose lives are less fortunate than yours. Give to others from your storehouse. Contribute some riches to close and trustworthy friends. And teach them the secret ways you attain things of value—both are precious. Use your human gifts to empathize with those who suffer, and your spiritual graces to show compassion to those who are afflicted. Graciously provide some treasures to righteous persons with a personal challenge or a just cause. Give good service to protect the defenseless, and creatively support "angels of rescue" who embrace this mission. Spread the Good News of God's salvation to everyone who is poor in spirit.

♦ financial, material, social, internal, intellectual, spiritual, and eternal things of value ♦

★ "[11] God replied: Solomon, you could have asked me to make you rich or famous or to let you live a long time. Or you could have asked for your enemies to be destroyed. Instead, you asked for wisdom and knowledge to rule my people. ¹² So I will make you wise and intelligent. But I will also make you richer and more famous than any king before or after you." (2 Chronicles 1:11–12, *CEV*)

✶ "^{29:11} Everyone was pleased with what I said and did. ¹² When poor people or orphans cried out for help, I came to their rescue. ¹³ And I was highly praised for my generosity to widows and others in poverty. ¹⁴ Kindness and justice were my coat and hat; ¹⁵ I was good to the blind and to the lame. ¹⁶ I was a father to the needy, and I defended them in court, even if they were strangers. ¹⁷ When criminals attacked, I broke their teeth and set their victims free. . . . ^{31:16} I have never cheated widows or others in need, ¹⁷ and I have always shared my food with orphans. ¹⁸ Since the time I was young, I have cared for orphans and helped widows. ¹⁹ I provided clothes for the poor, ²⁰ and I was praised for supplying woolen garments to keep them warm. . . . ²⁴ I have never trusted the power of wealth, ²⁵ or taken pride in owning many possessions." (Job 29:11–17; 31:16–20, 24–25, *CEV*)

✶ "¹⁰ They were thrilled and excited to see the star. ¹¹ When the men went into the house and saw the child with Mary, his mother, they knelt down and worshiped him. They took out their gifts of gold, frankincense, and myrrh and gave them to him." (Matthew 2:10–11, *CEV*)

✶ "If you give to others, you will be given a full amount in return. It will be packed down, shaken together, and spilling over into your lap. The way you treat others is the way you will be treated." (Luke 6:38, *CEV*)

✶ "^{32}My little group of disciples, don't be afraid! Your Father wants to give you the kingdom. ^{33}Sell what you have and give the money to the poor. Make yourselves moneybags that never wear out. Make sure your treasure is safe in heaven, where thieves cannot steal it and moths cannot destroy it. ^{34}Your heart will always be where your treasure is." (Luke 12:32–34, *CEV*)

✶ "^{1}Then, six days before the Passover, Jesus came to Bethany, where Lazarus was who had been dead, whom He had raised from the dead. ^{2}There they made Him a supper; and Martha served, but Lazarus was one of those who sat at the table with Him. ^{3}Then Mary took a pound of very costly oil of spikenard, anointed the feet of Jesus, and wiped His feet with her hair. And the house was filled with the fragrance of the oil." (John 12:1–3, *NKJV*)

★ "In everything I did, I showed you that by this kind of hard work we must help the weak, remembering the words the Lord Jesus himself said: 'It is more blessed to give than to receive.'"" (Acts 20:35, *NIV*)

★ "¹² no matter if that person is a Jew or a Gentile. There is only one Lord, and he is generous to everyone who asks for his help. ¹³ All who call out to the Lord will be saved." (Romans 10:12–13, *CEV*)

★ "and we are always happy, even in times of suffering. Although we are poor, we have made many people rich. And though we own nothing, everything is ours." (2 Corinthians 6:10, *CEV*)

★ "I am the least important of all God's people. But God was kind and chose me to tell the Gentiles that because of Christ there are blessings that cannot be measured." (Ephesians 3:8, *CEV*)

★ "¹⁷ Warn the rich people of this world not to be proud or to trust in wealth that is easily lost. Tell them to have faith in God, who is rich and blesses us with everything we need to enjoy life. ¹⁸ Instruct them to do as many good deeds as they can and to help everyone. Remind the rich to be generous and share what they have. ¹⁹ This will lay a solid foundation for the future, so that they will know what true life is like." (1 Timothy 6:17–19, *CEV*)

~ 10th ~

Show

your riches with discretion.

Discreetly display your wealth—your special gifts and goods. Reveal your treasures to others; show how you acquire your possessions. Disclose your valuables wisely (not foolishly) to deepen the worthwhile visions of those you trust. Uncover your resources to responsible persons, and in a manner that enriches their well-being and progress. Take care to reveal the hidden richness of your inner peace and the rich secrets to your spiritual strength—virtues sought by many.

◆ financial, material, social, internal, intellectual, spiritual, and eternal things of value ◆

✶ "[14] 'You are the light of the world. A town built on a hill cannot be hidden. [15] Neither do people light a lamp and put it under a bowl. Instead they put it on its stand, and it gives light to everyone in the house. [16] In the same way, let your light shine before others, that they may see your good deeds and glorify your Father in heaven." (Matthew 5:14–16, *NIV*)

✶ "[3] Joseph said to his brothers, 'I am Joseph! Is my father still living?' But his brothers were not able to answer him, because they were terrified at his presence. [4] Then Joseph said to his brothers, 'Come close to me.' When they had done so, he said, 'I am your brother Joseph, the one you sold into Egypt! [5] And now, do not be distressed and do not be angry with yourselves for selling me here, because it was to save lives that God sent me ahead of you. [6] For two years now there has been famine in the land, and for the next five years there will be no plowing and reaping. [7] But God sent me ahead of you to preserve for you a remnant on earth and to save your lives by a great deliverance. [8] 'So then, it was not you who sent me here, but God. He made me father to Pharaoh, lord of his entire household and ruler of all Egypt." (Genesis 45:3–8, *NIV*)

✶ "[1] At that time Marduk-Baladan son of Baladan king of Babylon sent Hezekiah letters and a gift, because he had heard of his illness and recovery. [2] Hezekiah received the envoys gladly and showed them what was in his storehouses—the silver, the gold, the spices, the fine olive oil—his entire armory and everything found among his treasures. There was nothing in his palace or in all his kingdom that Hezekiah did not show them. ³Then Isaiah the prophet went to King Hezekiah and asked, 'What did those men say, and where did they come from?' 'From a distant land,' Hezekiah replied. 'They came to me from Babylon.' ⁴The prophet asked, 'What did they see in your palace?' 'They saw everything in my palace,' Hezekiah said. 'There is nothing among my treasures that I did not show them.' ⁵Then Isaiah said to Hezekiah, 'Hear the word of the LORD Almighty: ⁶The time will surely come when everything in your palace, and all that your predecessors have stored up until this day, will be carried off to Babylon. Nothing will be left, says the LORD." (Isaiah 39:1–6, *NIV*)

✴ "²⁵At that time Jesus said, 'I praise you, Father, Lord of heaven and earth, because you have hidden these things from the wise and learned, and revealed them to little children. ²⁶Yes, Father, for this is what you were pleased to do." (Matthew 11:25–26, *NIV*)

✴ "⁹But you are a chosen people, a royal priesthood, a holy nation, God's special possession, that you may declare the praises of him who called you out of darkness into his wonderful light.¹⁰Once you were not a people, but now you are the people of God;

once you had not received mercy, but now you have received mercy." (1 Peter 2:9–10, *NIV*)

~ 11th ~
Sell
your riches for a profit.

Market your riches for others to buy, or to use in their life, work, or service. Use your riches to negotiate for better riches; trade them for your advantage. Employ your gifts of deep knowledge, wisdom, and experience to gain a profit, and to personally benefit from your immaterial treasures. Wholesale portions of your riches to obtain the best things of life; things that you truly need and deeply desire. Release certain possessions to receive things of greater wealth. Discount things of temporary value to gain blessings that will last. Unload earthly goods to redeem eternal treasures.

♦ financial, material, social, internal, intellectual, spiritual, and eternal things of value ♦

★ "[20] Jacob worked seven years for Laban, but the time seemed like only a few days, because he loved

Rachel so much. . . . ²⁸⁻³⁰ At the end of the week of celebration, Laban let Jacob marry Rachel, and he gave her his servant woman Bilhah. Jacob loved Rachel more than he did Leah, but he had to work another seven years for Laban." (Genesis 29:20, 28–30, *CEV*)

★ "She makes clothes to sell to the shop owners." (Proverbs 31:24, *CEV*)

★ "¹ Send your grain across the seas, and in time, profits will flow back to you. ² But divide your investments among many places, for you do not know what risks might lie ahead." (Ecclesiastes 11:1–2, *NLT*)

★ "⁴⁴ The kingdom of heaven is like what happens when someone finds treasure hidden in a field and buries it again. A person like that is happy and goes and sells everything in order to buy that field. ⁴⁵ The kingdom of heaven is like what happens when a shop owner is looking for fine pearls. ⁴⁶ After finding a very valuable one, the owner goes and sells everything in order to buy that pearl." (Matthew 13:44–46, *CEV*)

★ "Jesus looked closely at the man. He liked him and said, 'There's one thing you still need to do. Go sell everything you own. Give the money to the poor, and you will have riches in heaven. Then come with me.'" (Mark 10:21, *CEV*)

✶ "¹³ Now listen, you who say, 'Today or tomorrow we will go to this or that city, spend a year there, carry on business and make money.' ¹⁴ Why, you do not even know what will happen tomorrow. What is your life? You are a mist that appears for a little while and then vanishes. ¹⁵ Instead, you ought to say, 'If it is the Lord's will, we will live and do this or that.' ¹⁶ As it is, you boast in your arrogant schemes. All such boasting is evil. If anyone, then, knows the good they ought to do and doesn't do it, it is sin for them." (James 4:13–17, *NIV*)

~ 12th ~
Sprout
your riches to flourish.

Plant your riches to harvest more. Spawn spin-offs of riches to replenish your supply. Invest in new riches for an increase. Grow! Enrich the full fruition of your divine potential. Enjoy God's material and spiritual abundance as you sow occasional and eternal blessings. Flourish! Unceasingly renew the truest richness of your "blessful" life!

♦ financial, material, social, internal, intellectual, spiritual, and eternal things of value ♦

★ "⁴ Do not wear yourself out to get rich; do not trust your own cleverness. ⁵ Cast but a glance at riches, and they are gone, for they will surely sprout wings and fly off to the sky like an eagle." (Proverbs 23:4–5, *NIV*)

✶ "³ By wisdom a house is built, and through understanding it is established; ⁴ through knowledge its rooms are filled with rare and beautiful treasures." (Proverbs 24:3–4, *NIV*)

✶ "¹⁹ 'After a long time the master of those servants returned and settled accounts with them. ²⁰ The man who had received five bags of gold brought the other five. 'Master,' he said, 'you entrusted me with five bags of gold. See, I have gained five more.' ²¹ 'His master replied, 'Well done, good and faithful servant! You have been faithful with a few things; I will put you in charge of many things. Come and share your master's happiness!' ²² 'The man with two bags of gold also came. 'Master,' he said, 'you entrusted me with two bags of gold; see, I have gained two more.' ²³ 'His master replied, 'Well done, good and faithful servant! You have been faithful with a few things; I will put you in charge of many things. Come and share your master's happiness!'. . . . ²⁹ For whoever has will be given more, and they will have an abundance. Whoever does not have, even what they have will be taken from them." (Matthew 25:19–23, 29, *NIV*)

✶ "For you know the grace of our Lord Jesus Christ, that though he was rich, yet for your sake he became poor, so that you through his poverty might become rich." (2 Corinthians 8:9, *NIV*)

✶ "⁶ Remember this: Whoever sows sparingly will also reap sparingly, and whoever sows generously will also reap generously. ⁷ Each of you should give what you have decided in your heart to give, not reluctantly or under compulsion, for God loves a cheerful giver. ⁸ And God is able to bless you abundantly, so that in all things at all times, having all that you need, you will abound in every good work. ⁹ As it is written: 'They have freely scattered their gifts to the poor; their righteousness endures forever.' ¹⁰ Now he who supplies seed to the sower and bread for food will also supply and increase your store of seed and will enlarge the harvest of your righteousness. ¹¹ You will be enriched in every way so that you can be generous on every occasion, and through us your generosity will result in thanksgiving to God." (2 Corinthians 9:6–11, *NIV*)

✶ "And my God will meet all your needs according to the riches of his glory in Christ Jesus." (Philippians 4:19, *NIV*)

✶ "Beloved, I pray that you may prosper in all things and be in health, just as your soul prospers." (3 John 2, *NKJV*)

Here are the 12 principles
for gaining life's truest riches:

1. *Specify*	→ 2. *Sort*	→ 3. *Survey*	→ 4. *Sanctify*
→ 5. *Secure*	→ 6. *Shut Off*	→ 7. *Save*	→ 8. *Spend*
→ 9. *Share*	→ 10. *Show*	→ 11. *Sell*	→ 12. *Sprout*

Choose to work on those areas where you need the most improvement; ensure that your life will become enriched with the truest riches. Then, at the end of life's journey, my prayer is that your truest treasures may last eternally. The hymn below captures this spirit.

"Hold to God's Unchanging Hand"
by Jennie Wilson (1857–1913)

1. Time is filled with swift transition,
Naught of earth unmoved can stand,
Build your hopes on things eternal,
Hold to God's unchanging hand.

2. Trust in Him who will not leave you,
Whatsoever years may bring,
If by earthly friends forsaken
Still more closely to Him cling

3. Covet not this world's vain riches
   That so rapidly decay,
   Seek to gain the heav'nly treasures,
   They will never pass away.

4. When your journey is completed,
   If to God you have been true,
   Fair and bright the home in glory
   Your enraptured soul will view.

Refrain: Hold to God's unchanging hand,
Hold to God's unchanging hand;
Build your hopes on things eternal,
Hold to God's unchanging hand.

✝

"For God so loved the world that he gave his one and only Son, that whoever believes in him shall not perish but have eternal life."
(John 3:16, *NIV*)

✝

"Thanks be to God for his indescribable gift!"
(2 Corinthians 9:15, *NIV*)

✝

"Jesus Christ is the same yesterday and today and forever."
(Hebrews 13:8, *NIV*)